EASY LITERATURE-BASED QUILTS AROUND THE YEAR

✂

Reproducible Patterns and Writing Prompts
for 20 Collaborative Paper Quilts That Build
Important Literacy Skills and Brighten Up Your Classroom

◆

by Mariann Cigrand and Phyllis Howard

Scholastic Inc. grants teachers permission to photocopy the activity sheets from this book for classroom use. No other part of this publication may be reproduced in whole or in part, or stored in a retrieval system, or transmitted in any form or by any means, electronic, mechanical, photocopying, recording, or otherwise, without written permission of the publisher. For information regarding permission, write to Scholastic Inc., 555 Broadway, New York, NY 10012.

Cover design by Kelli Thompson
Interior design by Leah Bossio

ISBN # 0-439-13898-1
Copyright © 2000 by Mariann Cigrand and Phyllis Howard
All rights reserved.
Printed in the U.S.A.

Contents

A Note
From the Authors

"Reading is like a quilt—it is many pieces put together."

This is our philosophy. As Title I reading teachers for grades 1 to 3, it's our job to motivate students to read. To this end, we have been making literature-based paper quilts in our classroom for the past four years. We've discovered that our paper-quilt projects put a "hook" on good works of literature.

Children readily identify with a favorite blanket, as most of them have had one. Our paper quilts are blankets of favorite stories. In helping to construct them, children gain not only an understanding of how real quilts are made, but also an appreciation for good literature. The quilts motivate children to read more books, either by a particular author or on a particular subject.

Students eagerly ask about the next month's quilt project and often offer ideas and suggestions for upcoming books. They also try to predict what the quilt blocks might look like. Two years ago, we added writing responses to the quilts to encourage children to personally react to the literature and to stimulate higher-order thinking skills.

You may think that creating classroom quilts is a huge task, requiring a lot of time. Actually, making the quilts from beginning to end takes us only two 45-minute periods. To save time, we prepare quilting materials in advance. Sometimes we solicit volunteers and older students to help prepare the quilt pieces.

Each September, we see children struggle to put together the quilt-block pieces. By the end of the year, they have become experts at assembling the quilt pieces. We display our quilts in the hallway each month for students and staff members to enjoy. They often vote on their favorite quilt at the end of the year.

We believe that children at all grade levels would enjoy this project and gain from the experience of making paper quilts. We hope after using this book that you, too, will be hooked on quilting.

—*Mariann Cigrand and Phyllis Howard*

ABOUT THIS BOOK

What is a quilt? A quilt is a type of bed cover that consists of three layers: a patchwork top, a soft filling, and a plain back. The top of a quilt is often made from various pieces of materials sewn together. The colors, materials, and designs can be elaborate or simple. Either way, a quilt can be used as a venue for storytelling or as a work of art to hang in a museum.

In the last decade, teachers across America have been using quilts to teach a variety of subjects, including math, social studies, and literature. Quilts help teach patterns, measurement, calculations, and other math skills. Social-studies teachers use quilts to instruct students on different cultures. But quilts are most often used to teach literacy. Quilts provide an innovative way of telling a story.

This book will help you create a collaborative literature quilt in your classroom. After reading award-winning and much-loved children's books, children will assemble pieces of a quilt. They will delight in seeing their individual pieces come together to make the final product.

GETTING STARTED

If possible, bring in some real quilts to show students at the beginning of the year. Inform children that while quilts are generally made of cloth, their quilts will be made of paper.

Preparing Materials

• Photocopy quilt-block patterns for children to use beforehand.

• Precut all materials you need for the quilt-block pieces and store them in sealable bags. Cut all squares with a paper cutter. To make triangles, use scissors to cut the squares in half. You can use any material in any color or design you want. We suggest wallpaper, wrapping paper, and construction paper.

- Photocopy the design pattern for each selection on white paper for each child. Cut this white paper together with colored construction paper to make two patterns that match perfectly. (To find out what color paper to use for each pattern, read "Making the Quilt" under each selection.)

- Staple the matching patterns together along the upper edge, with the color paper on top. Children will write their response to the literature on the white paper.

Selecting the Book

- Each month, we provide you with two book options. Select the one that suits your particular needs or fits your current curriculum.

- We have provided before- and after-reading exercises that you can use to discuss the book with your students. Copy the writing prompts on the board. Invite students to select one prompt that they would like to complete and write it in the writing-response paper attached to their pattern block.

Assembling the Quilt

- Spaces on the quilt-block patterns are usually designated as 1, 2, etc. Students may have the option of choosing the color or pattern they want to use for the quilt. Sometimes, however, they have no choice. For example, the trees for December should always be green.

- Try adding a 3-D effect to the quilt blocks by gluing materials such as buttons, twigs, beads, or movable eyes. Tacky glue works best.

- Periodically, assess how students are doing with the quilt project. You may want to simplify some of the designs for younger students, or allow older students to cut out their own patterns to enrich their involvement with the project.

- To assemble a class quilt for display, keep each child's two quilt-block pieces together. This makes it easier to cut apart the pieces at the end of the year (see "Making Student Quilt Books," below). Use a paper cutter to trim all the quilt-block pieces to the same size. Glue the quilt blocks onto a large piece of butcher paper. Use construction-paper strips or commercial bulletin-board borders to decorate the quilt's borders.

Displaying Quilts
- Display the quilt for each month in the classroom or hallway, along with the book used for the quilt project. We usually leave our quilts up for the entire year.

- If space becomes a problem, take down the quilts and cut them apart to make individual quilt books for each student (see "Making Student Quilt Books," below).

Making Student Quilt Books
- At the end of the year, make a quilt book for each student to take home. Glue each child's quilt pieces for each month to 12-by-18-inch sheets of white construction paper, then bind the pages together. Write a short description of each book and quilt pattern to go with each page.

September

Launch a yearlong quilting project with one of two

classic picture books: *The Quilt Story* by Tony Johnston and

Tomie dePaola, and *The Keeping Quilt* by Patricia Polacco.

Set in separate times and places, both books convey the

significance of a homemade quilt to two different families.

◆

After reading, give children hands-on experience in putting

together their own easy-to-make patchwork paper quilt.

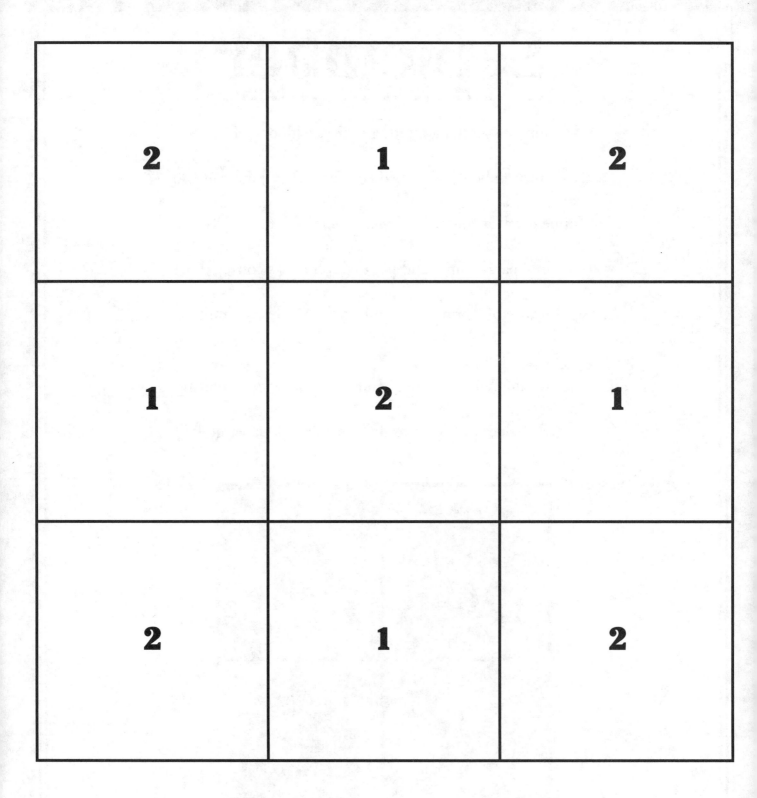

LET'S READ (Selection A)

The Quilt Story

by Tony Johnston and Tomie dePaola
(Putnam, 1985)

Summary: Abigail loves the quilt her mother makes for her. She nestles in it, plays with it, and sleeps with it wrapped around her. When her family moves, the quilt provides comfort and familiarity while everything else around her seems strange and new. Years later, another little girl rediscovers the quilt's warmth.

Before Reading: Ask students: What is a quilt? *(A quilt is a type of bed cover made with two layers of cloth and soft batting in between.)* Bring in various quilts to show children. Encourage them to take a close look at the different materials and patterns that make up the quilts. Inform students that quilts are made from scraps of different materials sewn together to create a pattern.

After Reading: Inform students that they will be making a paper quilt similar to the one in *The Quilt Story.* Each child will make two quilt blocks, which will then be glued together to create a class quilt.

Writing Prompts: Ask students to complete one of the following sentences to write in their paper quilt:

> • I would like my own quilt because _____.
>
> • I would use my quilt for _____.

Don't Stop Now!
After your class has finished making the paper quilt,

MAKING THE QUILT

You'll need (for each student):
◆ Nine-Patch Quilt Block pattern, page 10
◆ Nine 2 1/2-inch wallpaper squares (4 squares of one pattern and 5 squares of a coordinating pattern)
◆ House Block pattern, page 12, cut from white paper and colored construction paper (Give each child different-color construction paper, other than blue.)
◆ 7 1/2- inch square of blue construction paper (for background)
◆ Wooden bead
◆ 1-by-1 1/2-inch photo of student
◆ Glue

PIECE IT TOGETHER

1. To make the Nine-Patch Quilt Block, help students choose one wallpaper pattern for the spaces numbered "1," and a second, coordinating pattern for the spaces numbered "2." Have students glue the wallpaper squares onto the quilt block.

2. Give each child both House Block patterns stapled together. Have children write their response to the literature (from Writing Prompts, left) on the white paper house.

3. Have children glue the back of the white house to the center of the blue background square. Instruct students to glue their photos to the window of the colored house. To make a doorknob, have them glue a wooden bead to the door.

4. Assemble the class quilt. (See page 7 for instructions.)

inform students that they have just *collaborated*–worked together as a team–to create the class quilt. Explain that authors and illustrators also collaborate to create storybooks. Divide your class into pairs. Assign one child in each pair to be the author and the other, the illustrator. Challenge each pair to collaborate on a short storybook about the child in the house block.

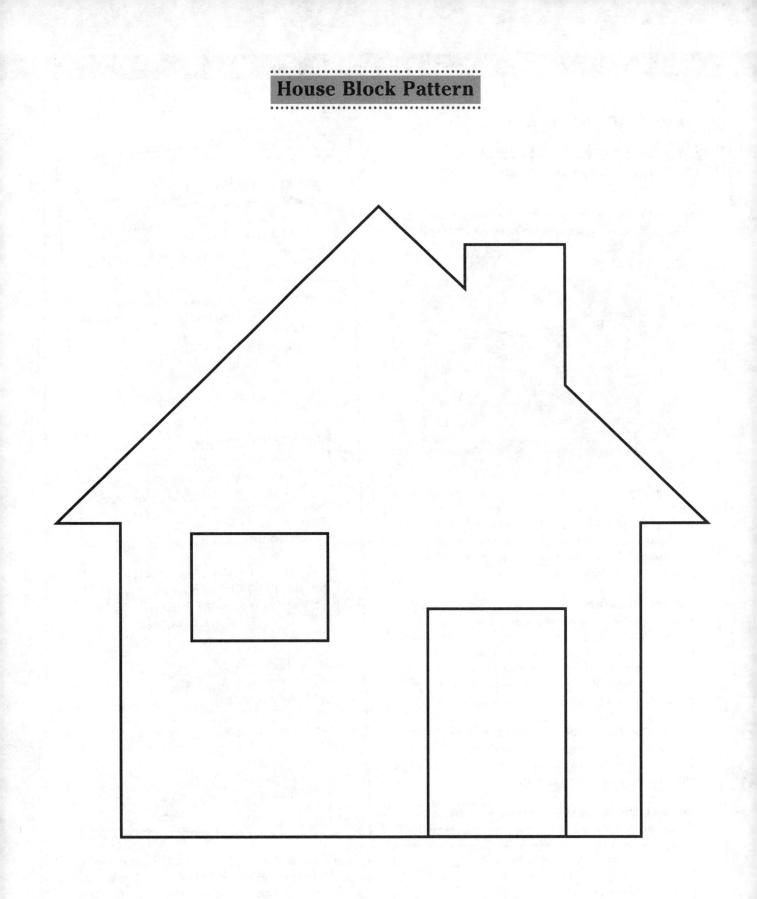

LET'S READ (Selection B)

The Keeping Quilt

by Patricia Polacco
(Simon & Schuster, 1994)

Summary: When Anna's family moves from Russia to America, her mother makes a quilt out of old clothes to help remember and celebrate their rich heritage. As the quilt passes from generation to generation, it serves as a wedding canopy, a baby blanket, a Sabbath tablecloth, and more.

Before Reading: Encourage children to imagine what it must feel like to move to a new place. Explain to them that a new place doesn't have to be a new country, or even a new town. It could be a new classroom or even a new place to sit in class. Ask students: How does it feel to be in a new place?

After Reading: Inform students that, like the Keeping Quilt, many quilts are made from scraps of cloth that have special meaning or memories. Invite students to think about what they would like to include in a quilt if they were to make one.

Writing Prompts: Ask students to complete one of the following sentences to write in their paper quilt:

> • The one piece I would put in my quilt would come from _____ because _____.
>
> • I think quilts can be important to a family because _____.

MAKING THE QUILT

You'll need (for each student):

- ◆ Nine-Patch Quilt Block pattern, page 10
- ◆ Nine 2 1/2-inch wallpaper squares (4 squares of one pattern and 5 squares of a coordinating pattern)
- ◆ Tulip Block pattern, page 14, cut from white paper and colored construction paper (Give each child different-color construction paper, other than light blue.)
- ◆ Two leaves, page 14, cut from green construction paper
- ◆ 3-inch green pipe cleaner
- ◆ 7 1/2-inch square of light-blue construction paper (for background)
- ◆ Glue

PIECE IT TOGETHER

1. To make the Nine-Patch Quilt Block, help students choose one wallpaper pattern for the spaces numbered "1," and a second, coordinating pattern for the spaces numbered "2." Have students glue the wallpaper squares onto the quilt block.

2. Give each child both Tulip Block patterns stapled together. Have children write their response to the literature (from Writing Prompts, left) on the white tulip.

3. Have students glue the back of the white tulip near the top of the light-blue background square. Then have them glue the pipe cleaner to the tulip to make a stem. Finally, glue the leaves near the bottom of the stem.

4. Assemble the class quilt. (See page 7 for instructions.)

Don't Stop Now!

The quilt that Anna's family creates in *The Keeping Quilt* is an *heirloom*–something valuable handed from one generation to the next. Have students interview their family to find out about any family heirlooms, such as a watch, a toy, or even a blanket. Then invite children to share stories about their heirloom.

October

In this month, when spooky stories abound, follow the spine-tingling

adventure of a boy and his sister as they try to conquer their fear

of *The Ghost-Eye Tree*. If you prefer to stay away from

the traditional Halloween fare, the story of *Stellaluna*, a bat adopted

by a family of birds, offers a more benign alternative.

◆

To reflect on this month's theme, students create

a class quilt using a Bat Quilt Block and a Tree Block pattern.

2	2	2	2 / 1	1
2	2	2	1	2
2	2	1	2	2
2 / 1	1	2	2	2
1	2	2	2	2

LET'S READ (Selection A)

The Ghost-Eye Tree
by Bill Martin Jr. and John Archambault
(Henry Holt, 1988)

Summary: A mother sends a boy and his sister to fetch a bucket of milk at the end of town at night. Halfway there, they walk by the Ghost-Eye Tree, a huge, eerie, old oak tree. The poetry of this book enhances the spooky imaginings of the boy and his sister.

Before Reading: Ask children: Have your parents ever asked you to do something that made you feel scared? For example, getting something from the basement, or going to the doctor. Was it as scary as you thought it would be? Inform students that they will read a story about a boy and his sister who try to overcome their fear of a big, old tree.

After Reading: Encourage children to think about what they would do if they were in the same situation as the boy and his sister.

Writing Prompts: Ask students to complete one of the following sentences to write in their paper quilt:

> • If I saw a Ghost-Eye Tree I would _____.
>
> • I would _____ so I won't have to go for milk.

Don't Stop Now!
The relationship between the boy and his sister is an integral part of *The Ghost-Eye Tree*. Divide students into

MAKING THE QUILT
You'll need (for each student):
- Bat Quilt Block pattern, page 16
- Six 1 1/2-inch squares of black construction paper (Cut one square in half to make two triangles.)
- Nineteen 1 1/2-inch squares of orange or yellow construction paper* (Cut one square in half to make two triangles.)
- Two small orange or yellow circles (Punch out the circles, from construction paper.)
- Tree Block pattern, page 18, cut from brown construction paper
- 5 1/2-by-6 1/2-inch black construction paper
- 5 1/2-by-6 1/2-inch white paper
- 7 1/2-inch square of brown construction paper (for background)
- Two small, movable eyes
- Glue
- Stapler

*Give half the class yellow construction paper, and the other half, orange.

PIECE IT TOGETHER
1. To make the Bat Quilt Block, have students glue the black squares and triangles to the spaces numbered "1" to form the bat, and the orange or yellow squares and triangles to the spaces numbered "2." Have children glue orange or yellow circles to the center "bat" square to make bat eyes.

2. Have children glue the tree to the center of the black construction paper. Then glue the movable eyes to the tree.

3. Instruct students to write their response to the literature (from Writing Prompts, left) on the white paper. Then help them staple the black paper with the tree to the white paper, along the top.

4. Have children glue the back of the white paper to the brown background square.

5. Assemble the class quilt. (See page 7 for instructions.)

pairs and invite them to act out the parts of the boy and his sister.

LET'S READ (Selection B)

Stellaluna
by Janell Cannon
(Harcourt Brace, 1993)

Summary: After an owl attacks, Stellaluna, a baby bat, becomes separated from her mother and is adopted by a family of birds. Stellaluna soon gives up her bat ways and behaves like a good little bird–until she meets her mother again.

Before Reading: Show students pictures of bats and birds. Ask students: How are bats and birds the same? (*Both animals have wings and can fly.*) How are they different? (*Bats are mammals–they are covered with fur and give birth to live young. Birds have feathers and lay eggs.*) Tell students that you will read a story about a bat that grows up thinking she is a bird. As you read the story, have students make a mental list of other similarities and differences between birds and bats.

After Reading: Ask students: What do you think is the most important lesson Stellaluna and the baby birds learn? (*No matter how different friends can be, they can still be alike in many ways.*)

Writing Prompts: Ask students to complete one of the following sentences to write in their paper quilt:

> • My friend and I are alike because _____ and we are different because _____.
>
> • I would like to teach my friend how to _____.

Don't Stop Now!

Read the books *Horace* by Holly Keller (Greenwillow, 1991) and *A Mother for Choco* by Keiko Kasza (Putnam, 1992) to students. Both books feature a child

MAKING THE QUILT
You'll need (for each student):
◆ Bat Quilt Block pattern, page 16
◆ Six 1 1/2-inch squares of brown construction paper (Cut one square in half to make two triangles.)
◆ Nineteen 1 1/2-inch squares of blue construction paper (Cut one square in half to make two triangles.)
◆ Two small black circles (Punch out the circles from construction paper.)
◆ Tree Block pattern, page 18, cut from black construction paper
◆ 5 1/2-by-6 1/2-inch blue construction paper
◆ 5 1/2-by-6 1/2-inch white paper
◆ 7 1/2-inch square of brown construction paper (for background)
◆ Straw
◆ Glue
◆ Stapler

PIECE IT TOGETHER

1. To make the Bat Quilt Block, have students glue the brown squares and triangles to the spaces numbered "1" to form the bat, and the blue squares and triangles to the spaces numbered "2." To make "bat eyes," have children glue black circles to the center "bat" square.

2. Have children glue the tree to the center of the blue construction paper. Then have them make a small straw nest and glue it to the tree.

3. Instruct students to write their response to the literature (from Writing Prompts, left) on the white paper. Then help them staple the blue paper with the tree to the white paper.

4. Have children glue the back of the white paper to the brown background square.

5. Assemble the class quilt. (See page 7 for instructions.)

that looks different from its parents. Ask children: Do you think it's important that a child looks like its parents? Why or why not?

November

Introduce students to the richness of Native American culture
with this month's book selections. In *Knots on a Counting Rope*,
a young blind boy finds guidance and strength in his grandfather.
Legend of the Indian Paintbrush tells the story of a boy destined
to be different from others in his tribe.

◆

A simple Diamond-in-Square Quilt block provides an
elegant backdrop for Native American symbols.

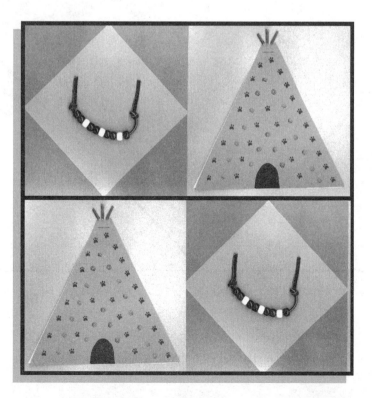

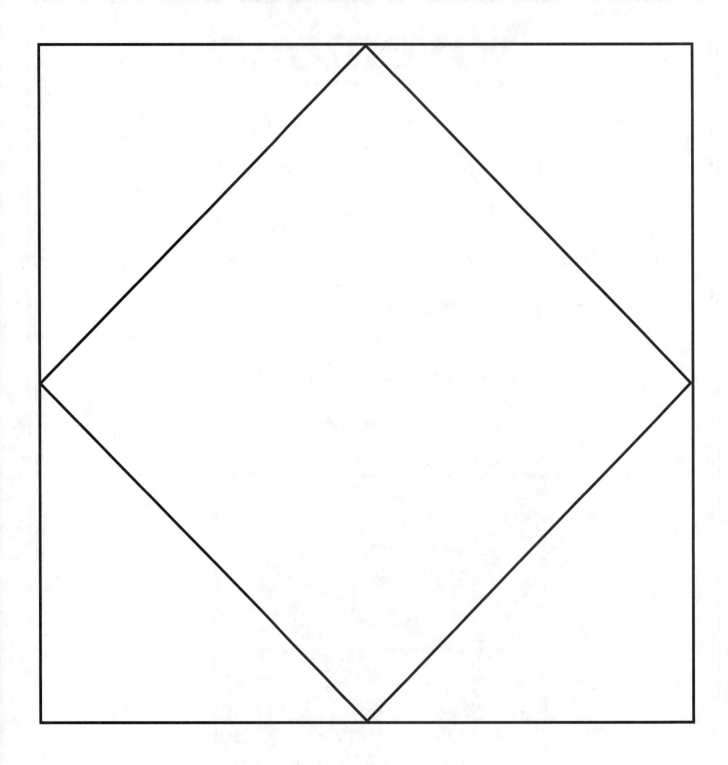

LET'S READ (Selection A)

Knots on a Counting Rope

by Bill Martin Jr. and John Archambault
(Henry Holt, 1987)

Summary: A Native American boy asks his grandfather to tell him again the story of his birth and his name. To help the blind boy understand the passage of time, his grandfather adds a knot to a counting rope each time he repeats the story.

Before Reading: To help students experience what it's like to be blind, have them close their eyes or blindfold them. Then have students try to walk around a designated area, eat snacks, or fill a glass of water. Help them understand that being blind doesn't mean being helpless.

After Reading: Explain to students that the grandfather helps and encourages the boy to overcome the challenges of being blind. Ask students: Who in your life helps and encourages you to be the best person you can be? Can you name 10 people who are important in your life?

Writing Prompts: Ask students to complete one of the following sentences to write in their paper quilt:

- Ten important people in my life are _____.

- Even if I were blind, I would _____.

MAKING THE QUILT
You'll need (for each student):
- Diamond-in-Square Quilt Block pattern, page 22
- 5-inch square of light-blue construction paper
- 7-inch square of brown construction paper
- Ten different-color beads
- 10-inch piece of leather lacing
- Tepee Block pattern, page 24, cut from white paper and brown construction paper
- 7-inch square of light-blue construction paper (for background)
- Three small twigs
- Ink stamps of Indian symbols
- Glue
- Stapler

PIECE IT TOGETHER
1. To make the Diamond-in-Square Quilt Block, have students glue the 5-inch blue square to the 7-inch brown square so that the blue square forms a diamond on top of the brown square.

2. Have children string 10 beads on the leather lacing. Then help them staple the string of beads to the center of the blue triangle, as shown.

3. Give each child both Tepee Block patterns stapled together. Then have the children write their response to the literature (from Writing Prompts, left) on the white tepee.

4. Have students glue the back of the white tepee to the center of the blue background paper. Have students glue twigs to the top of the tepee and draw a door. Then encourage children to decorate their tepees using ink stamps of Indian symbols.

5. Assemble the class quilt. (See page 7 for instructions.)

Don't Stop Now!
In *Knots on a Counting Rope*, the blind boy owns a horse that serves as "his eyes." Have children think about ways in which animals help people. For example, seeing-eye dogs help blind people cross the streets. Invite students to write a short story about an animal that helps people.

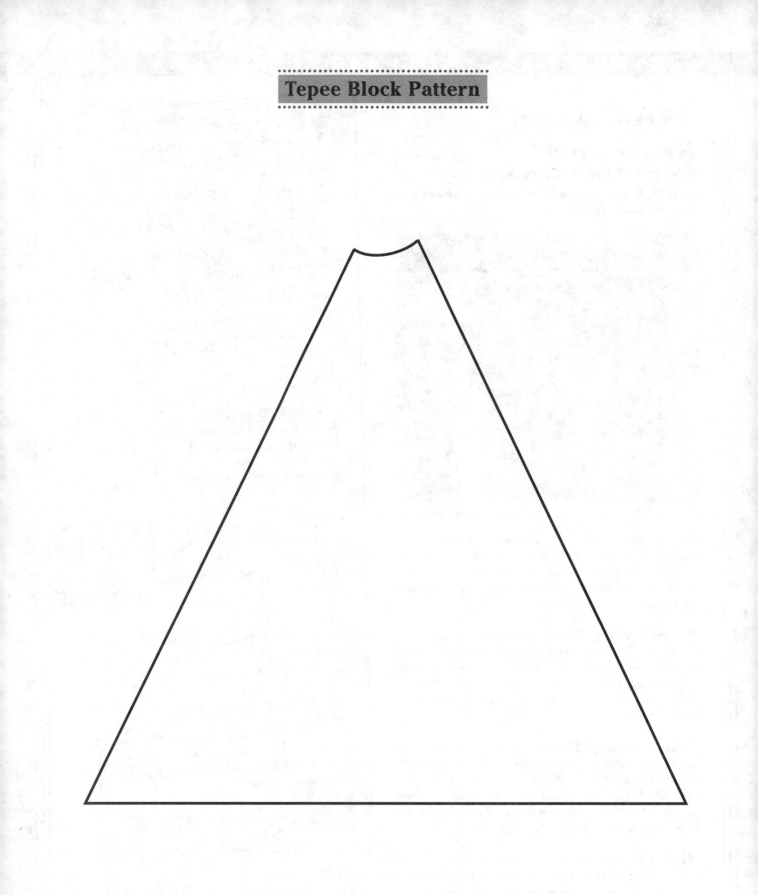

LET'S READ (Selection B)

The Legend of the Indian Paintbrush

by Tomie dePaola
(Putnam, 1988)

Summary: This book retells an Indian legend in which a small boy cannot keep up with other boys in his tribe. Then he learns in a dream vision that he is destined for other greatness–he will paint the legends of his people.

Before Reading: Ask students: What is a legend? (*A legend is a story of some wonderful event that has been passed down for generations.*) Explain to students that, unlike a myth, a legend may be based on a historical event. As you read the book, have students think about whether or not the story really happened.

After Reading: Invite children to think about things they do very well (for example, paint, sing, or play basketball). Ask them: What is something you can do that you're proud of?

Writing Prompts: Ask students to complete one of the following sentences to write in their paper quilt:

> • One great talent I have is _____.
>
> • My dream-vision is _____.

Don't Stop Now!

Divide the class into groups of four. Encourage each group to create a legend based on something that

MAKING THE QUILT

You'll need (for each student):
◆ Diamond-in-Square Quilt Block pattern, page 22
◆ 5-inch square of light-blue construction paper
◆ 7-inch square of brown construction paper
◆ Ten different-color beads
◆ 10-inch piece of leather lacing
◆ Animal Skin Block pattern, page 26, cut from white paper and brown construction paper
◆ 7-inch square of blue construction paper (for background)
◆ Crayons or markers
◆ Glue
◆ Stapler

PIECE IT TOGETHER

1. To make the Diamond-in-Square Quilt Block, have students glue the 5-inch blue square to the 7-inch brown square so that the blue square forms a diamond on top of the brown square.

2. Have children string 10 beads on the leather lacing. Then help them staple the string of beads to the center of the blue triangle, as shown.

3. Give each child both Animal Skin Block patterns stapled together. Then have the children write their response to the literature (from Writing Prompts, left) on the white animal skin.

4. Have students glue the back of the white animal skin to the blue background square. Invite children to use crayons or markers to draw Indian symbols on the brown animal skin.

5. Assemble the class quilt. (See page 7 for instructions.)

actually happened in class. For example, how the guinea pig came to be the class pet.

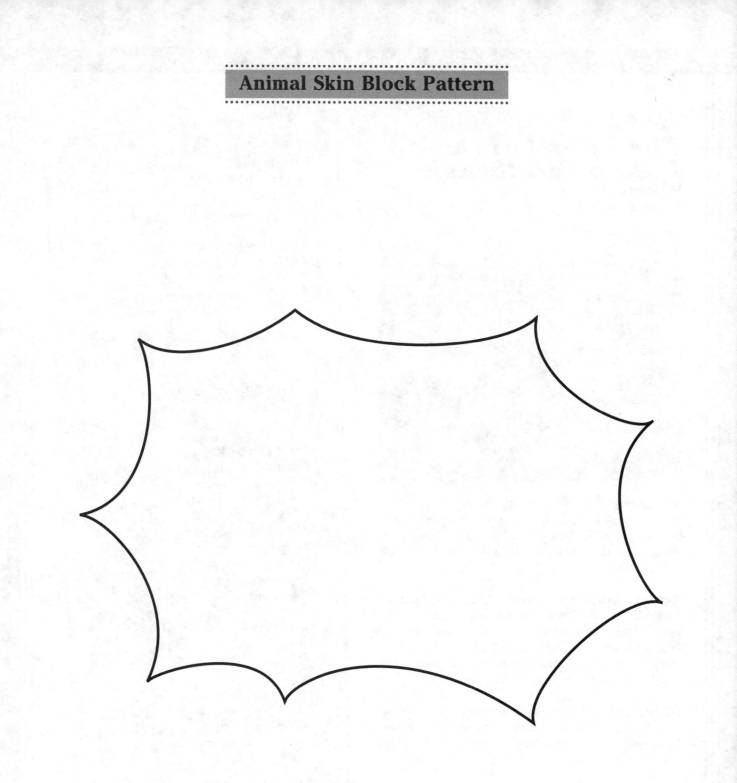

December

Celebrate the holiday season with *The Polar Express*, a story about a

boy's first Christmas gift. *North Country Night*, our second selection,

doesn't focus on holidays, but rather on the winter season. Set in a forest covered

with snow, the book introduces readers to the world of nocturnal animals.

◆

Whether as a traditional Christmas tree or an ordinary pine tree,

this month's Tree Quilt Block pattern helps students identify

the central theme in both books.

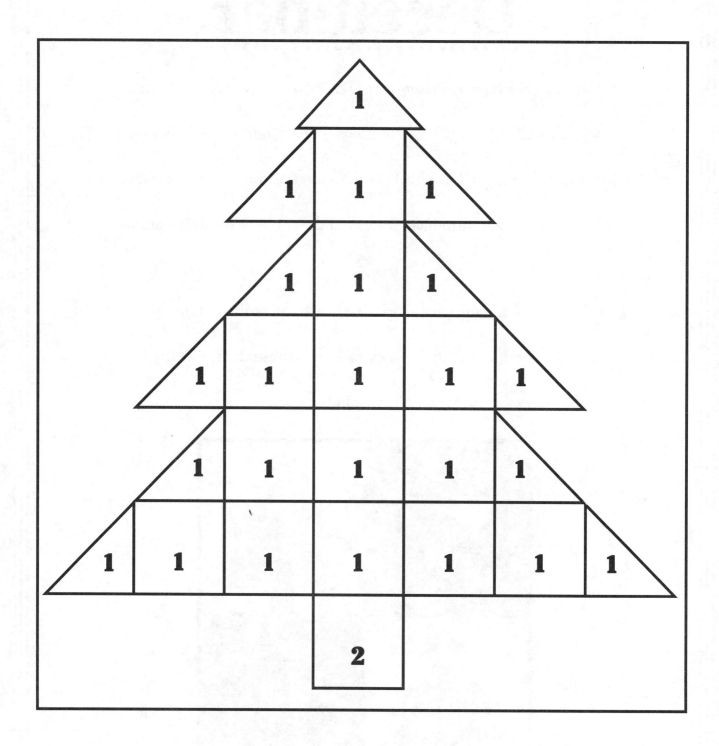

LET'S READ (Selection A)

The Polar Express
by Chris Van Allsburg
(Houghton Mifflin, 1985)

Summary: A boy's belief in Santa Claus secures him a spot on The Polar Express, a magical train to the North Pole. When he arrives there, the boy receives the first gift of Christmas from Santa–a silver bell that can be heard only by those who believe.

Before Reading: Find out how many students have been on a train. Encourage children to share their experience. Set up chairs in the classroom to resemble a train. Then invite children to "climb aboard" and listen as you read the story. You may also want to bring in a jingle bell to ring during the story.

After Reading: Ask students: Of all the gifts the boy could ask for, why do you think he asked for a silver bell? What would you have asked for?

Writing Prompts: Ask students to complete one of the following sentences to write in their paper quilt:

> • For my first gift of Christmas, I would want
> _____.
>
> • The part of the story that I liked best is
> _____.

MAKING THE QUILT
You'll need (for each student):
◆ Tree Quilt Block pattern, page 28
◆ Nineteen 1-inch squares of green metallic paper (Cut six squares in half to make 12 triangles. You'll use only 11.)
◆ 1-inch square of black construction paper
◆ Gold star
◆ Train Block pattern, page 30, cut from white paper and black construction paper
◆ 7-inch square of red construction paper (for background)
◆ 1-by-1 1/2-inch white paper
◆ 1-by-1-inch photo of student
◆ Small jingle bell, attached to a short red ribbon
◆ Glue

PIECE IT TOGETHER
1. To make the Tree Quilt Block, have children glue the green squares and triangles to spaces numbered "1," and the black square to the space numbered "2." Have students glue the star to the top of the tree.

2. Give each child both Train Block patterns stapled together. Then have the children write their response to the literature (from Writing Prompts, left) on the white train.

3. Have children glue the back of the white train to the center of the red background square. Then have them glue the 1-by-1 1/2-inch white window to the black train. Finally, have them glue their photo to the window, as well as the jingle bell.

4. Assemble the class quilt. (See page 7 for instructions.)

Don't Stop Now!
In December, people celebrate different holidays. Create a Holiday Graph of different holidays, including birthdays, your students celebrate on a large piece of craft paper. Graph the number of students who celebrate each holiday or event.

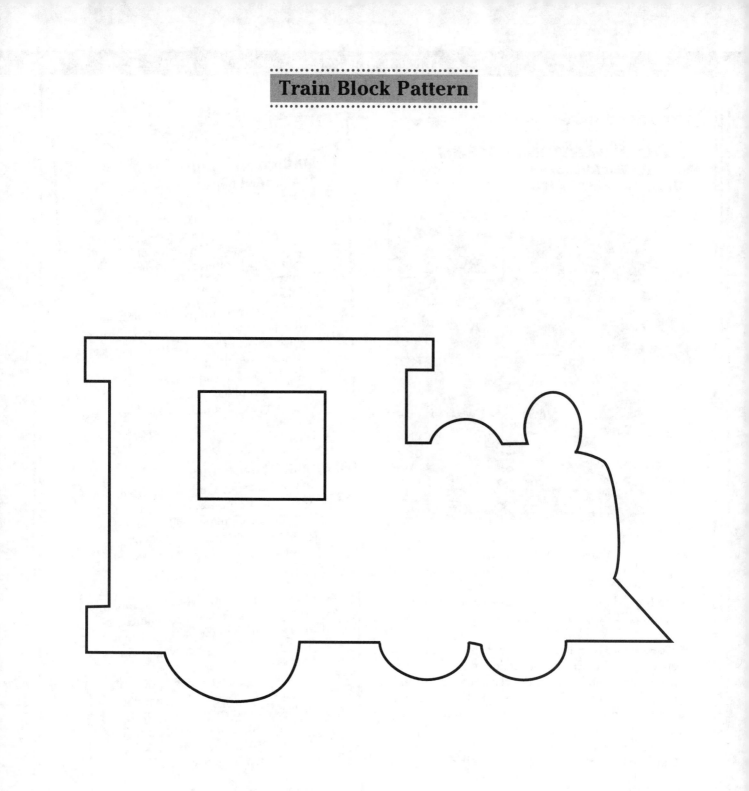

LET'S READ (Selection B)

North Country Night
by Daniel San Souci
(Picture Yearling, 1994)

Summary: In the North Country, after people have gone to sleep, night animals such as owls, coyotes, and raccoons awake. They prowl, stalk, search for food, or try to stay safe from a predator. Beautiful illustrations enhance this glimpse of a snow-covered setting from dusk till dawn.

Before Reading: Challenge students to name some animals that sleep during the day and awaken at night. (*Owls, raccoons, etc.*) Ask: What do you think these animals do at night when they wake up? (*Look for food, escape predators, etc.*)

After Reading: Invite children to share what they have learned about nighttime animals.

Writing Prompts: Ask students to complete one of the following sentences to write in their paper quilt:

• I learned that nighttime creatures _____.

• My favorite nighttime animal is the _____ because _____.

Don't Stop Now!
Copy the two columns here on a board. Then invite students to match each animal from *North Country Night* to its safe place.

Animal	Safe Place
Porcupine	Brush
Beaver	Den
Owl	Woodchuck's burrow
Fox	Tree
Weasel	Lodge

MAKING THE QUILT
You'll need (for each student):

◆ Tree Quilt Block pattern, page 28
◆ Nineteen 1-inch squares of green construction paper (Cut six squares in half to make 12 triangles. You'll use only 11.)
◆ 1-inch square of light-brown construction paper
◆ White glitter
◆ Owl Block pattern, page 32, cut from white paper and light-brown construction paper
◆ 7-inch square of black construction paper (for background)
◆ Triangular beak, page 32, cut from yellow construction paper
◆ Two oval eyes, page 32, cut from dark-brown construction paper
◆ Yellow crayon
◆ Two large, movable eyes
◆ Glue

PIECE IT TOGETHER

1. To make the Tree Quilt Block, have children glue the green squares and triangles to spaces numbered "1," and the black square to the space numbered "2." Have children smear a thin layer of glue on the tree, then sprinkle glitter on it.

2. Give each child both Owl Block patterns stapled together. Then have the children write their response to the literature (from Writing Prompts, left) on the white owl.

3. Have students glue the back of the white owl to the center of the black background square. Then have them glue the dark-brown oval eyes to the owl, and glue the movable eyes to the ovals. Finally, have children glue the yellow beak to the owl and use the yellow crayon to draw its legs.

4. Assemble the class quilt. (See page 7 for instructions.)

Owl Block Pattern

January

Raymond Briggs's fantastical book *The Snowman* will bring children's

imagination to life as they follow a boy's adventures

with his snowman. Children will also enjoy exploring the wonders

of winter with young Peter in Ezra Jack Keats's *The Snowy Day.*

◆

The Flying-Geese Quilt Block pattern elicits images of geese flying

in V formation as they migrate south for the winter–a perfect

complement to the classic winter patterns of a snowman and a snowflake.

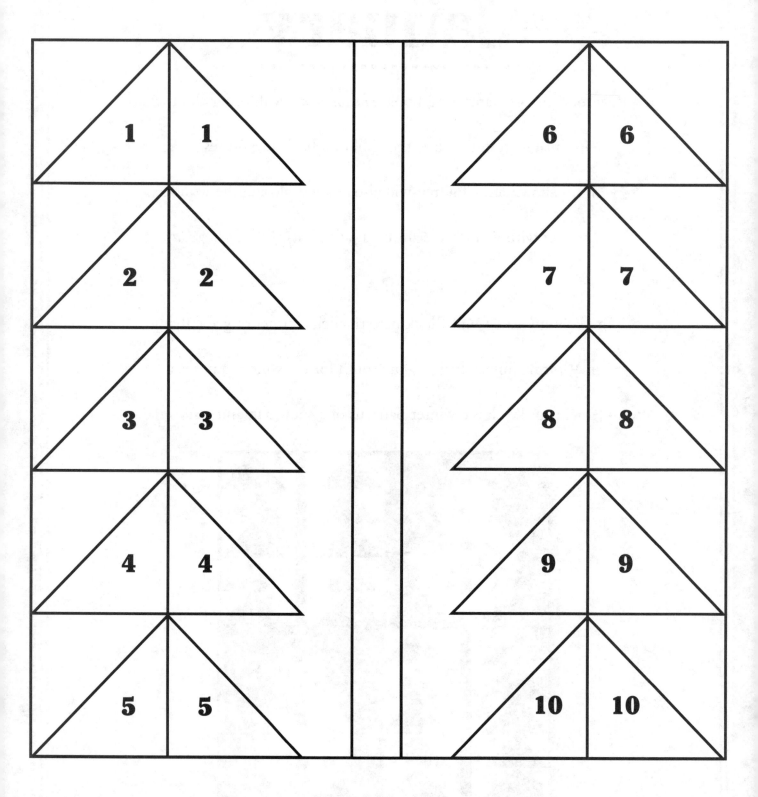

LET'S READ (Selection A)

The Snowman

by Raymond Briggs
(Random House, 1989)

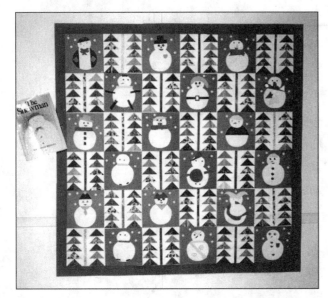

Summary: In this picture book without words, a boy builds a snowman, watches it come to life, then joins it on a magical adventure. When the boy awakens the next morning, he discovers that his snowman has melted.

Before Reading: Ask children: Do you think a book can tell a story without words? (*Yes*) Explain to students that you're about to "read" them a story with no words. Ask children to think about why the author chose to use only pictures, and no words, to tell his story.

After Reading: Ask children: Do you think the boy's adventures with the snowman were real, or just a dream? Why do you think so?

Writing Prompts: Ask students to complete one of the following sentences to write in their paper quilt:

> • If a snowman came into my house, I would _____.
>
> • I think the story is true (or not true) because _____.

Don't Stop Now!

Divide the class into pairs. Challenge each pair to work together to write words that would go in each picture frame of *The Snowman*. Ask them: What do you think the snowman and the boy are saying in each picture? Then invite children to read aloud what they've written.

MAKING THE QUILT

You'll need (for each student):

◆ Flying-Geese Quilt Block pattern, page 34
◆ Ten 1 1/2-inch squares of various wallpaper patterns (Cut each square in half to make triangles.)
◆ 1/2-by-7 1/2-inch strip of wallpaper
◆ Two Snowman Block patterns, page 36, cut from white paper
◆ 7 1/2-inch square of dark-blue construction paper (for background)
◆ Sequin snowflakes, or snowflakes made using snowflake paper punch
◆ Different-color construction paper (to decorate snowman)
◆ Glue
◆ Scissors

PIECE IT TOGETHER

1. To make the Flying-Geese Quilt Block, help students choose one wallpaper pattern for each of the spaces numbered "1" to "10." Have students glue the wallpaper triangles onto the quilt block, and the wallpaper strip to the center of the block.

2. Give each child both Snowman Block patterns stapled together. Have children write their response to the literature (from Writing Prompts, left) on the second snowman.

3. Have students glue the back of the snowman to the center of the blue background paper. Then have them add snowflakes to the background.

4. Encourage children to decorate their snowman using different-color construction paper. They could cut out a hat, eyes, a mouth, a nose, a scarf, and buttons, and glue them to their snowman.

5. Assemble the class quilt. (See page 7 for instructions.)

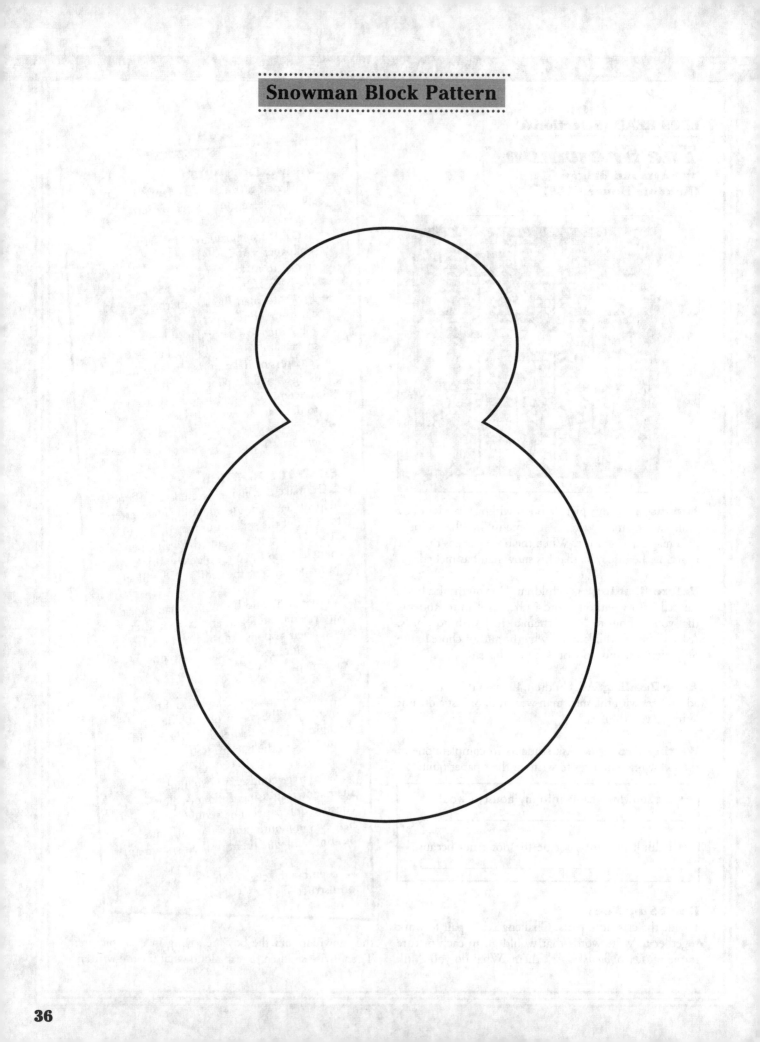

LET'S READ (Selection B)

The Snowy Day
by Ezra Jack Keats
(Viking Press, 1981)

Summary: Peter awakens to a world of snow. Excited, he bundles up and makes tracks, creates snow angels, goes sliding, and packs snowballs. At the end of this wonderful day, Peter saves a snowball in his pocket to remember what fun he had.

Before Reading: Ask children if they have seen snow. Encourage them to describe snow. Ask children: What do you like most about snow? What do you like least?

After Reading: Encourage children to share their own story about what they would like to do on a snowy day.

Writing Prompts: Ask students to complete one of the following sentences to write in their paper quilt:

> • On a snowy day, I like to _____.
>
> • I do (or do not) like snow because _____.

Don't Stop Now!
Invite students to pretend they're snowflakes falling to the ground. Call out different words or scenarios for kids to follow. For example, have children pretend to be a snowflake swirling around in a windy day, or several tiny flakes joining together to form a larger snowflake. Encourage children to think of other ways in which snowflakes might fall.

MAKING THE QUILT
You'll need (for each student):
◆ Flying-Geese Quilt Block pattern, page 34
◆ Ten 1 1/2-inch squares of various wallpaper patterns (Cut each square in half to make triangles.)
◆ 1/2-by-7 1/2-inch strip of wallpaper
◆ 5-inch square of white paper (to make a snowflake)
◆ 6 1/2-inch square of dark-blue construction paper
◆ 6 1/2-inch square of white paper
◆ 7 1/2-inch square of dark-blue construction paper (for background)
◆ White glitter
◆ Glue
◆ Scissors
◆ Stapler

PIECE IT TOGETHER
1. To make the Flying-Geese Quilt Block, help students choose one wallpaper pattern for each of the spaces numbered "1" to "10." Have students glue the wallpaper triangles onto the quilt block, and the wallpaper strip to the center of the block.

2. To make a snowflake, have students fold and cut their 5-inch white square, as shown on page 38.

3. Help children glue the snowflake to the center of the 6 1/2-inch dark-blue square. Have them smear a thin layer of glue on the snowflake, then sprinkle glitter on it.

4. Have children write their response to the literature (from Writing Prompts, left) on the white paper. Staple the white paper to the back of the blue paper with snowflake. Then glue the back of the white paper to the 7 1/2-inch square of dark-blue construction paper.

5. Assemble the class quilt. (See page 7 for instructions.)

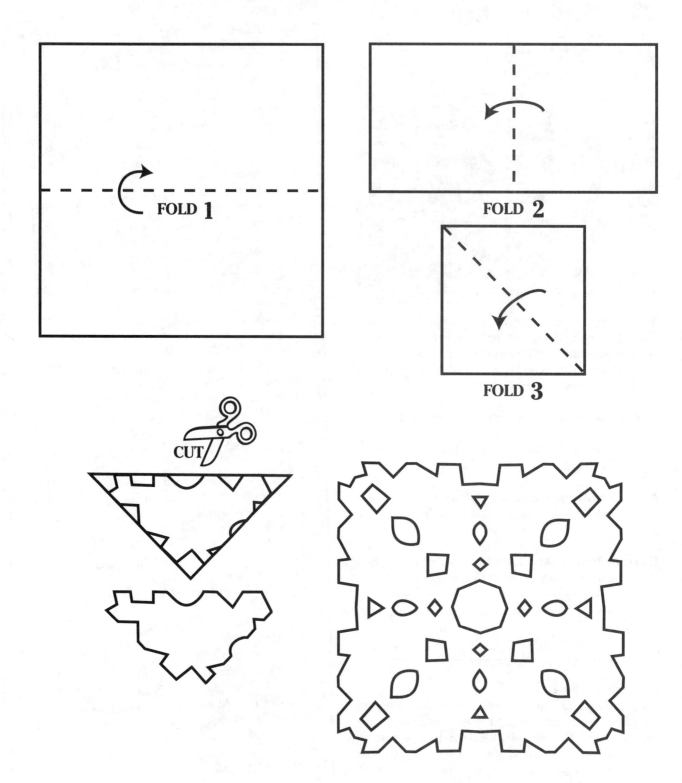

FOLD **1**

FOLD **2**

FOLD **3**

CUT

February

Warm children's hearts with a story set in Alaska about

a young girl and her mother, who reassures her child

of her unconditional love. You can also take this opportunity

to introduce children to one of this nation's

greatest presidents, Abraham Lincoln.

◆

This month's Sawtooth Star Quilt Block provides

a wonderful complement to the heart and Lincoln patterns.

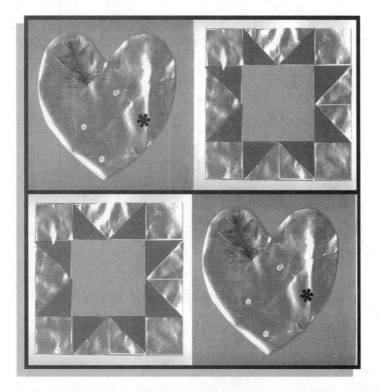

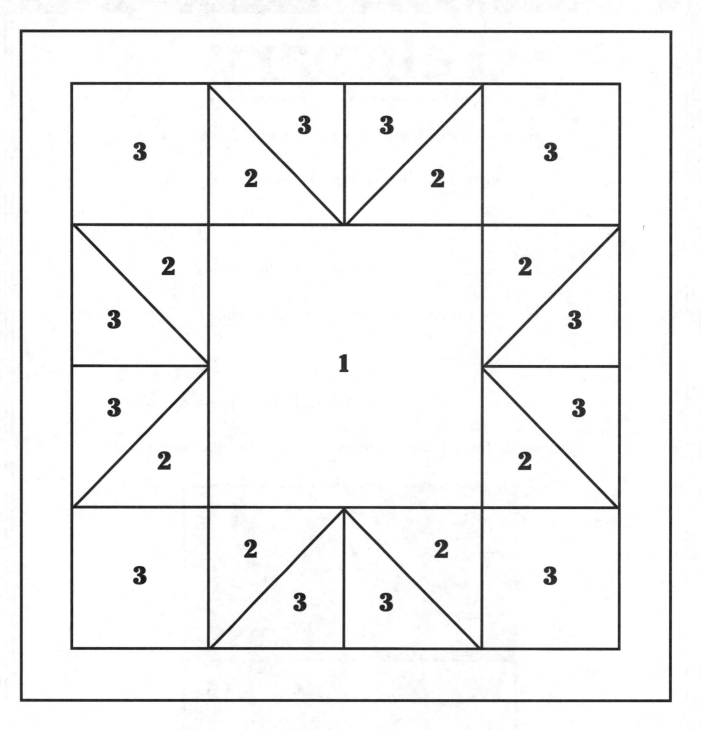

LET'S READ (Selection A)

Mama, Do You Love Me?
by Barbara M. Joosse
(Chronicle Books, 1991)

Summary: A young girl in Alaska asks her mother if she loves her. As the mother tries to reassure her, the little girl asks, what if she put salmon in her mother's parka, or turned into a polar bear. No matter how outlandish the child's imagined scenarios, her mother remains steadfast in her love.

Before Reading: Show children where they can find Alaska on a map. Inform them that even though Alaska seems far away, it is part of the United States. Bring in pictures of Alaska, including its people and animals, to share with students.

After Reading: The concept of parents loving their child is universal. Have students think of ways in which their parents show their love for them.

Writing Prompts: Ask students to complete one of the following sentences to write in their paper quilt:

• I know my mother (or father) loves me because
_____.

• I love my mother (or father) more than
a _____ loves _____.

Don't Stop Now!

Many of the animals mentioned in the book are found only in Alaska. Challenge students to change the setting of the story (for example, in their own town or

state) and rewrite the story to include animals that can be found only in the environment they selected.

MAKING THE QUILT
You'll need (for each student):

◆ Sawtooth Star Quilt Block pattern, page 40
◆ 3-inch square of pink construction paper
◆ Four 1 1/2-inch squares of purple construction paper* (Cut the squares in half to make triangles.)
◆ Eight 1 1/2-inch squares of silver wrapping paper* (Cut four squares in half to make eight triangles.)
◆ Heart Block pattern, page 42, cut from white paper and silver wrapping paper
◆ 7-inch square of pink construction paper for background
◆ Sequins, spangles, and feathers (to decorate hearts)
◆ Glue

*Switch the number of squares of purple construction paper and silver wrapping paper for half of your class. This way, half the quilt blocks will have silver star spokes and the other half will have purple star spokes.

PIECE IT TOGETHER

1. To make the Sawtooth Star Quilt block, have children glue the 3-inch pink square to the space numbered "1," the purple (or silver) triangles to the spaces numbered "2," and the silver (or purple) squares and triangles to the spaces numbered "3."

2. Give each child both Heart Block patterns stapled together. Then have the children write their response to the literature (from Writing Prompts, left) on the white heart.

3. Have children glue the back of the white heart to the 7-inch pink background square. Invite children to decorate their hearts using sequins, feathers, and other small objects.

4. Assemble the class quilt. (See page 7 for instructions.)

LET'S READ (Selection B)

A. Lincoln and Me
by Louise Borden
(Scholastic, 1999)

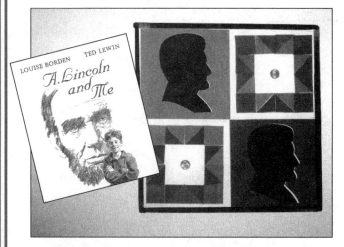

Summary: A young boy, who shares the same birthday as Abraham Lincoln, reminisces about the famous president. The boy feels a strong attachment to Lincoln, and finds comfort in the fact that, like him, Lincoln was tall, skinny, and clumsy. Even though Lincoln was called names such as "gorilla" and "baboon," he still proved himself to be one of the nation's greatest leaders.

Before Reading: Ask students: Do you know who Abraham Lincoln was? (*He was the 16th president of the United States.*) Explain to students that Abraham Lincoln helped end slavery and kept the country together during a bitter war between the Northern and Southern states. He was later killed by a man who disagreed with his views.

After Reading: Discuss with students the different things the boy liked about Abraham Lincoln. Ask: What do you like about Abraham Lincoln?

Writing Prompts: Ask students to complete one of the following sentences to write in their paper quilt:

• I admire Abraham Lincoln because _____.

• I wish I could have asked Abraham Lincoln _____.

Don't Stop Now!
The month of February is packed with holidays:

MAKING THE QUILT
You'll need (for each student):
◆ Sawtooth Star Quilt Block pattern, page 40
◆ Four 1 1/2-inch squares of red construction paper* (Cut each square in half to make triangles.
◆ Eight 1 1/2-inch squares of dark-blue construction paper* (Cut four squares in half to make eight triangles.)
◆ One Lincoln penny
◆ Lincoln Silhouette Block pattern, page 44, cut from white paper and black construction paper
◆ 7-inch square red or dark-blue construction paper (for background)
◆ Glue

*Switch the number of squares of red and dark-blue construction paper for half of your class. This way, half the quilt blocks will have red star spokes and the other half will have blue star spokes.

PIECE IT TOGETHER
1. To make the Sawtooth Star Quilt Block, have children glue the red (or blue) triangles to the spaces numbered "2," and the blue (or red) squares and triangles to the spaces numbered "3." Have students glue the Lincoln penny on top of the number "1" in the center square.

2. Give each child both Lincoln Silhouette Block patterns stapled together. Then have the children write their response to the literature (from Writing Prompts, left) on the white silhouette.

3. Have children glue the back of the white silhouette to the red or dark-blue background square.

4. Assemble the class quilt. (See page 7 for instructions.)

Presidents' Day, Valentine's Day, and often a winter school break. Invite children to invent a holiday to be celebrated in February. Then throw a party to celebrate it.

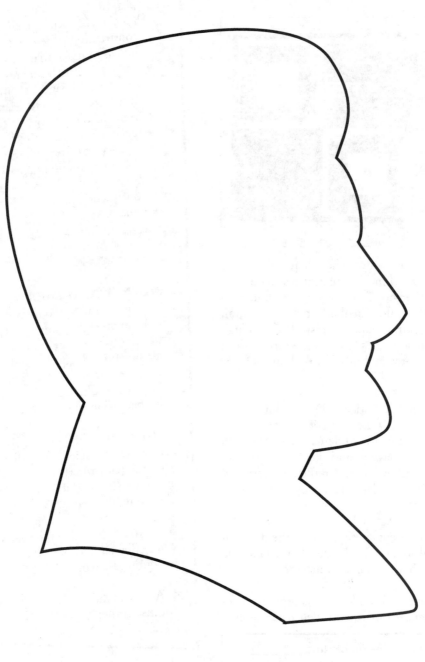

MARCH

Jan Brett's classic picture book *The Mitten* offers a final

tribute to winter with the story of a lost mitten that becomes

home to many woodland animals. To celebrate Saint Patrick's Day

in spring, share the amusing story of

Clever Tom and the Leprechaun with your students.

◆

The Pinwheel Quilt Block pattern is reminiscent

of March's windy days.

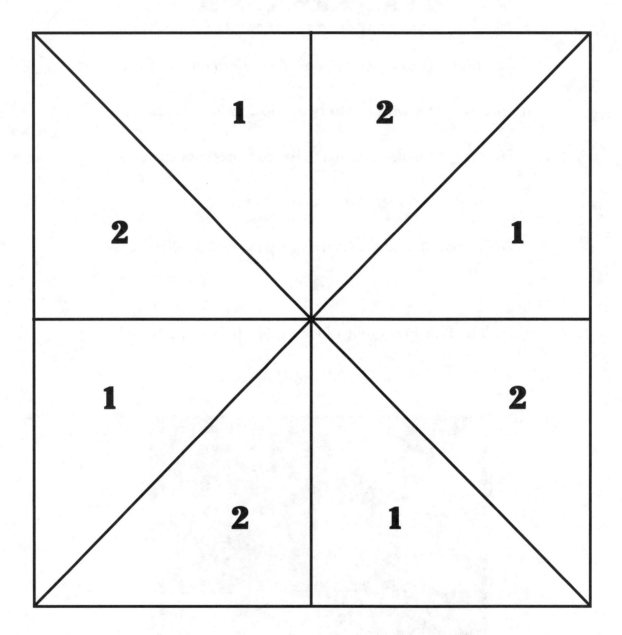

LET'S READ (Selection A)

The Mitten
by Jan Brett
(Putnam, 1989)

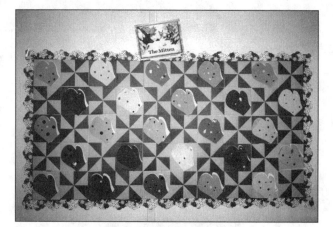

Summary: In this adaptation of a Ukrainian folk tale, a boy named Nicki begs his grandmother to knit him white mittens. His grandmother warns Nicki that he might lose his mittens in the snow–and he does. The missing mitten becomes home to more and more woodland animals, including a big brown bear who sneezes. Into the air pops the mitten, and falls right back into Nicki's hand!

Before Reading: Bring in an old knit mitten to show children. Pass the mitten around so students can test its stretchability. Ask them: Do you think a rabbit can fit inside the mitten? (*Maybe*) How about a bear? (*No*) Inform students that you will now read a story about a mitten that becomes a temporary home to many animals.

After Reading: Encourage children to imagine what would happen to their mitten if they lost it somewhere.

Writing Prompts: Ask students to complete one of the following sentences to include in their paper quilt:

- I lost my mitten at (or in) _____ and a _____ crawled into it.

- If animals used my mitten as a home, _____.

MAKING THE QUILT
You'll need (for each student):
- Pinwheel Quilt Block pattern, page 46
- Two 3-inch squares of blue construction paper (Cut each square in half to make triangles.)
- Two 3-inch squares of yellow construction paper (Cut each square in half to make triangles.)
- Mitten Block pattern, page 48, cut from white paper and colored construction paper (Give each child a different-color construction paper, but not blue or yellow.)
- 6-inch square of blue or yellow construction paper (for background)
- Sequins for decorating mitten
- Glue

PIECE IT TOGETHER
1. To make the Pinwheel Quilt Block, have students glue the blue (or yellow) triangles in the spaces numbered "1," and the yellow (or blue) triangles in the spaces numbered "2."

2. Give each child both Mitten Block patterns stapled together. Then have the children write their response to the literature (from Writing Prompts, left) on the white mitten.

3. Have children glue the back of the white mitten to the yellow or blue background paper. Invite children to decorate their mittens with sequins.

4. Assemble the class quilt. (See page 7 for instructions.)

Don't Stop Now!
Challenge students to guess how many marbles a mitten could hold. Then, one by one, drop a marble into the mitten until it can't hold any more. Count each marble as you drop it. How many marbles fit in the mitten?

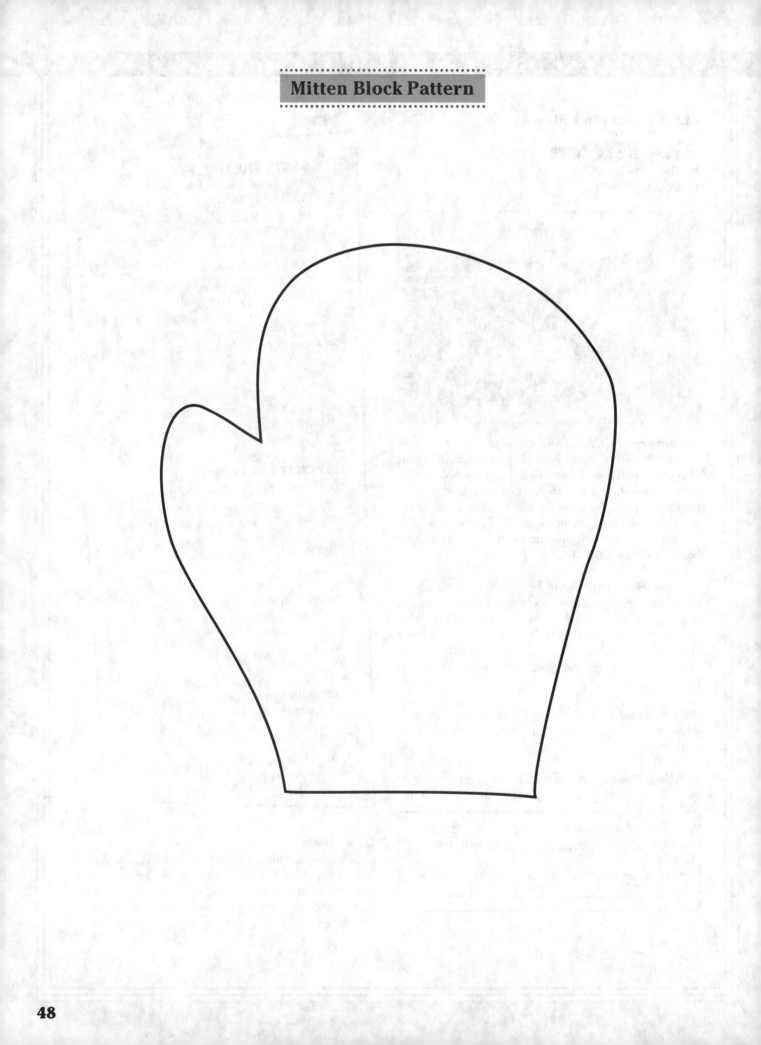

LET'S READ (Selection B)

Clever Tom and the Leprechaun
by Linda Shute
(Scholastic, 1990)

Summary: When Tom meets a leprechaun, he knows just what to do. After all, Tom is clever and knows all about leprechauns. He knows that they each have a pot of gold, and that they never lie. But just how clever is Tom? Is he clever enough to get the leprechaun's gold, or is the leprechaun even trickier than Tom?

Before Reading: Ask children if they have ever heard of a leprechaun. Inform them that a leprechaun is an imaginary character in Irish folklore. The tiny leprechaun can be merry one moment, mischievous and tricky the next. Legends say that if you capture a leprechaun, you can trick him into telling you where he has hidden his pot of gold.

After Reading: Ask children: If you caught a leprechaun, what would you ask for?

Writing Prompts: Ask students to complete one of the following sentences to write in their paper quilt:

> • I would catch a leprechaun by _____.
>
> • If I found a pot of gold I would _____.

Don't Stop Now!
Divide your class into small groups and encourage each group to produce a play based on *Clever Tom and the Leprechaun*. Assign play writers, scenery and prop people, and actors. Limit the plays to one or two pages.

MAKING THE QUILT
You'll need (for each student):
◆ Pinwheel Quilt Block pattern, page 46
◆ Two 3-inch squares of green construction paper (Cut each square in half to make triangles.)
◆ Two 3-inch squares of yellow construction paper (Cut each square in half to make triangles.)
◆ Shamrock Block pattern, page 50, cut from white paper and green construction paper
◆ 6-inch square of yellow construction paper (for background)
◆ Gold-covered chocolate coin
◆ Glue

PIECE IT TOGETHER
1. To make the Pinwheel Quilt Block, have students glue the green (or yellow) triangles in the spaces numbered "1," and the yellow (or green) triangles in the spaces numbered "2."

2. Give each child both Shamrock Block patterns stapled together. Then have the children write their reponse to the literature (from Writing Prompts, left) on the white shamrock.

3. Have children glue the back of the white shamrock to the yellow background square. Then have them glue the gold-covered chocolate coin to the center of the shamrock.

4. Assemble the class quilt. (See page 7 for instructions.)

APRIL

Bunnies and eggs may remind kids of Easter, but this month's

two selections teach valuable lessons to your students.

The Runaway Bunny reinforces the theme of a mother's

enduring love, while the story of *The Talking Eggs* teaches

a lasting lesson in kindness and humility.

◆

Students will enjoy completing the complex pattern of

this month's Basket Quilt Block pattern.

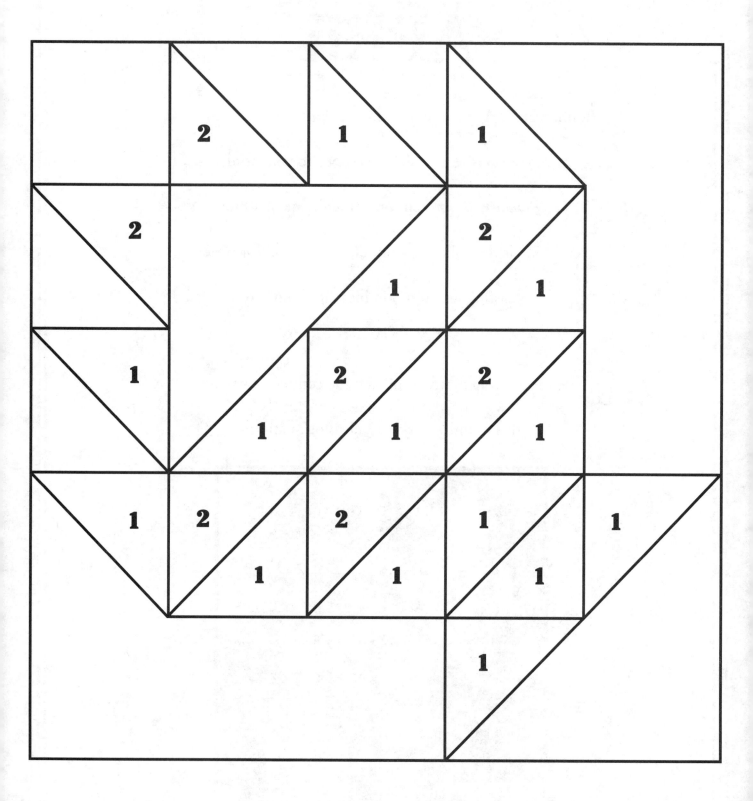

LET'S READ (Selection A)

The Runaway Bunny
by Margaret Wise Brown
(HarperTrophy, 1977)

Summary: A little bunny tells his mother that he is running away. As the bunny spins stories of different ways in which he'll try to escape or hide from her, his mother tells him how she will find him and love him.

Before Reading: Ask children if they have ever thought of running away. Stress to children that running away is never a good idea. Parents get worried, and children could get hurt or lost. They should talk to their parents or teachers instead.

After Reading: In the story, the little bunny imagines himself as various objects hiding in different places. Have children think of other ways the bunny could hide.

Writing Prompts: Ask students to complete one of the following sentences to write in their paper quilt:

> • If I were a _____, my mother (or father) would find me by _____.
>
> • My mother (or father) does _____ to show she (or he) loves me.

Don't Stop Now!
Ask students: Why do you think the illustrator drew some pictures in black and white? (*Black-and-white*

MAKING THE QUILT
You'll need (for each student):

◆ Basket Quilt Block pattern, page 52
◆ Eight 1 1/2-inch squares of light-green construction paper* (Cut each square in half to make triangles. You'll have one triangle left over.)
◆ Four 1 1/2-inch squares of pink construction paper* (Cut each square in half to make triangles. You'll have one triangle left over.)
◆ Easter grass
◆ Two Bunny Block patterns, page 54, cut from white paper
◆ 7 1/2-inch square of pink or light-green construction paper (for background)
◆ Cotton ball for bunny tail
◆ Glue

*Switch the number of squares of light-green and pink construction paper for half of your class. This way, half the quilt blocks will have pink baskets and the other half will have light-green baskets.

PIECE IT TOGETHER
1. To make the Basket Quilt Block, have students glue the light-green (or pink) triangles to the spaces numbered "1," and the pink (or light-green) triangles to the spaces numbered "2." Have children glue Easter grass to the large triangle below the basket's "handle."

2. Give each child both Bunny Block patterns stapled together. Then have the children write their response to the literature (from Writing Prompts, left) on the second bunny.

3. Have children glue the back of the bunny to the pink or light-green background paper. Glue the cotton-ball tail to the bunny.

4. Assemble the class quilt. (See page 7 for instructions.)

pictures of the bunny running away emphasize the sadness of each situation.) Invite students to redraw the black-and-white illustrations with colors.

LET'S READ (Selection B)

The Talking Eggs
by Robert D. San Souci
(Dutton, 1989)

Summary: Blanche's mother and sister force her to work hard, while they enjoy themselves. When Blanche helps a strange, old woman, the woman rewards her generously with talking eggs that turn into rubies, diamonds, coins, and more. Hoping to gain the same fortune, Blanche's sister searches for the old woman. Will she get her just reward?

Before Reading: Remind children of the story of Cinderella. Ask students: What kind of a person is Cinderella? (*She's good, kind, and hard-working.*) What about her stepmother and stepsisters? (*They're selfish, lazy, and unkind.*) Inform children that the book *The Talking Eggs* is similar to the story of Cinderella. As they listen to or read the book, have them think about how the characters are like those in Cinderella.

After Reading: Ask children: If you could ask the talking eggs for anything in the world, what would you ask for?

Writing Prompts: Ask students to complete one of the following sentences to include in their paper quilt:

> • If I found talking eggs, I would _____.
>
> • I would like the talking eggs to give me _____ because _____.

Don't Stop Now!

Invite children to make their own jeweled "talking eggs." Have each child bring in a hard-boiled egg from home. Then invite them to decorate their eggs using glue, sequins, gems, and markers.

MAKING THE QUILT

You'll need (for each student):

◆ Basket Quilt Block pattern, page 52
◆ Eight 1 1/2-inch squares of light-green construction paper* (Cut each square in half to make triangles. You'll have one triangle left over.)
◆ Four 1 1/2-inch squares of pink construction paper* (Cut each square in half to make triangles. You'll have one triangle left over.)
◆ Easter grass
◆ Egg Block pattern, page 56, cut from white paper and gold or silver wrapping paper
◆ 7 1/2-inch square of light-green or pink construction paper (for background)
◆ Sequins
◆ Glue

*Switch the number of squares of light-green and pink construction paper for half of your class. This way, half the quilt blocks will have pink baskets and the other half will have light-green baskets.

PIECE IT TOGETHER

1. To make the Basket Quilt Block, have students glue the light-green (or pink) triangles to the spaces numbered "1," and the pink (or light-green) triangles to the spaces numbered "2." Have children glue Easter grass to the large triangle below the basket's "handle."

2. Give each child both Egg Block patterns stapled together. Then have the children write their response to the literature (from Writing Prompts, left) on the white egg.

3. Have children glue the back of the white egg to the pink or light-green background paper. Encourage them to decorate their eggs with sequins.

4. Assemble the class quilt. (See page 7 for instructions.)

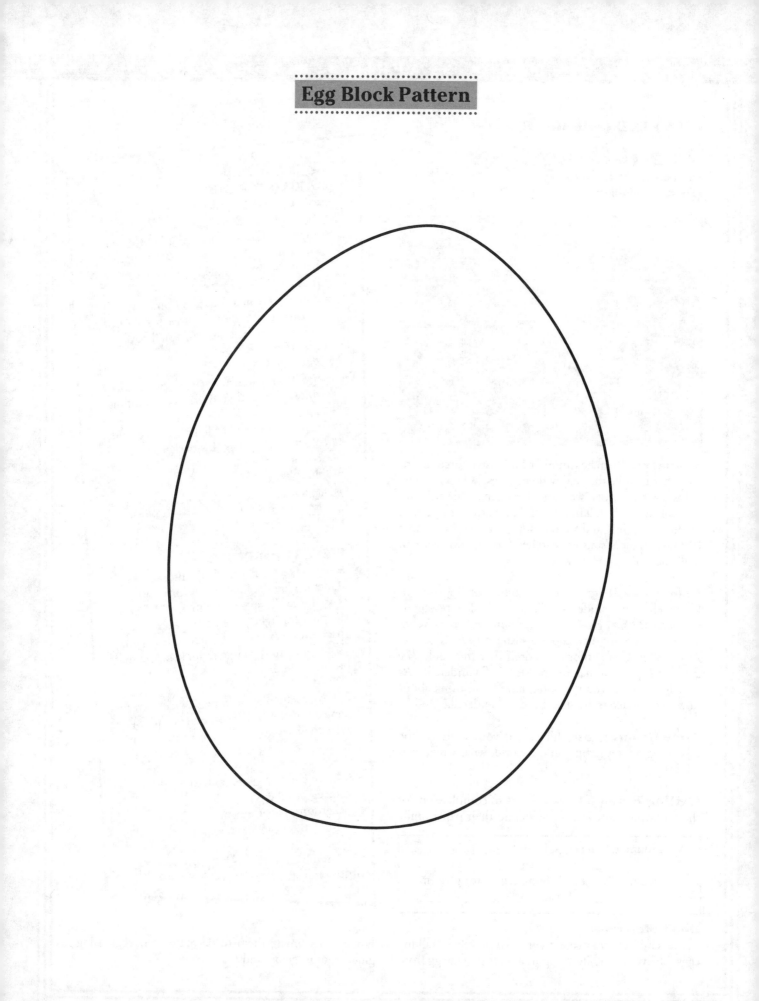

Egg Block Pattern

MAY

As the weather gets warmer and flowers bloom, children will enjoy

reading the story about a little girl who creates a special

flower box just for her mother. A visit to the rain forest may also

intrigue students as they meet different animals that make

their home in a giant kapok tree.

◆

Students will find the bright, colorful patterns

of this month's quilt appealing.

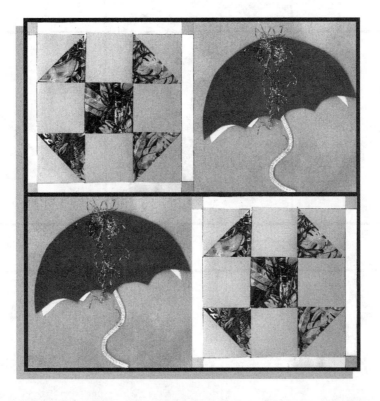

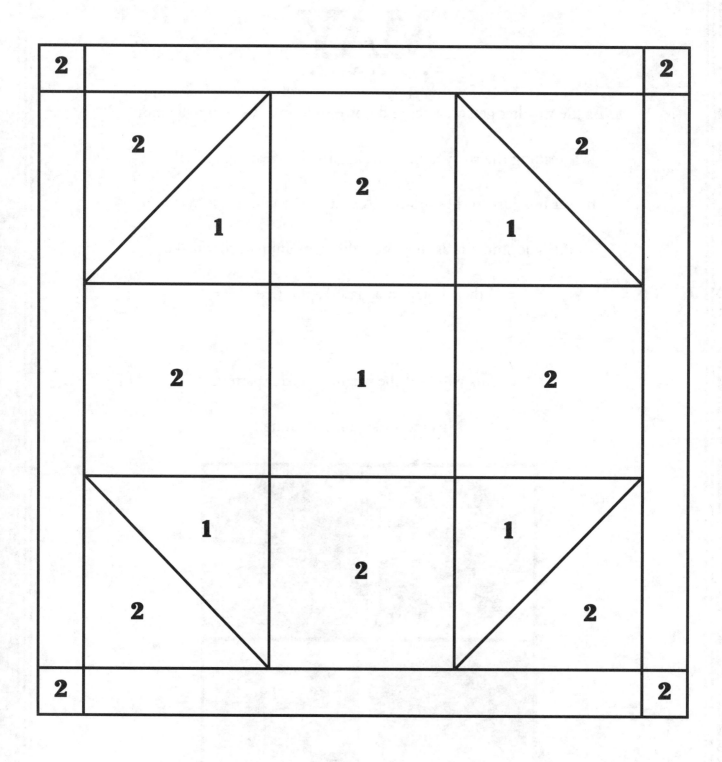

LET'S READ (Selection A)

The Great Kapok Tree
by Lynne Cherry
(Harcourt Brace, 1990)

Summary: A man comes into the rain forest to chop down the great kapok tree. As the man takes a nap beneath the tree, the animals that live in it invade his sleep and plead with him to save their tree.

Before Reading: Read aloud the author's note at the beginning of the book. The note provides information about the Amazon rain forest and what happens when rain forests are destroyed. Show children the map following the author's note and point out how much of the world's rain forests have already been destroyed.

After Reading: Ask children: Do you think we should try to save the rain forest? Why or why not?

Writing Prompts: Ask students to complete one of the following sentences to include in their paper quilt:

> • We should save the rain forest because _____.
>
> • I would like to visit a rain forest because _____.

Don't Stop Now!
Invite students to create a "Save the Rain Forest" poster. Have them draw animals from the book with speech bubbles. Have students write what each animal would say to convince the reader to save their home.

MAKING THE QUILT
You'll need (for each student):
- Philadelphia Pavements Quilt Block pattern, page 58
- Three 2-inch squares of flower- or jungle-print wrapping paper (Cut two squares in half to make four triangles.)
- Six 2-inch squares of yellow or red construction paper* (Cut two squares in half to make four triangles.)
- Four 1/2-inch squares of yellow or red construction paper
- Umbrella Block pattern, page 60, cut from white paper and red or yellow construction paper
- 7-inch square of green construction paper (for background)
- 4-inch white pipe cleaner
- Tinsel
- Glue

*Give half the class yellow construction paper, and the other half, red.

PIECE IT TOGETHER
1. To make the Philadelphia Pavements Quilt Block, have students glue the flower- or jungle-print squares and triangles to the spaces numbered "1," and the yellow or red squares and triangles to the spaces numbered "2."

2. Give each child both Umbrella Block patterns stapled together. Have children write their response to the literature (from Writing Prompts, left) on the white umbrella.

3. Have students glue the back of the white umbrella near the top of the green background square. Then have them shape the pipe cleaner into an umbrella handle and glue it to the umbrella. Have children add tinsel to the umbrella to represent rain.

4. Assemble the class quilt. (See page 7 for instructions.)

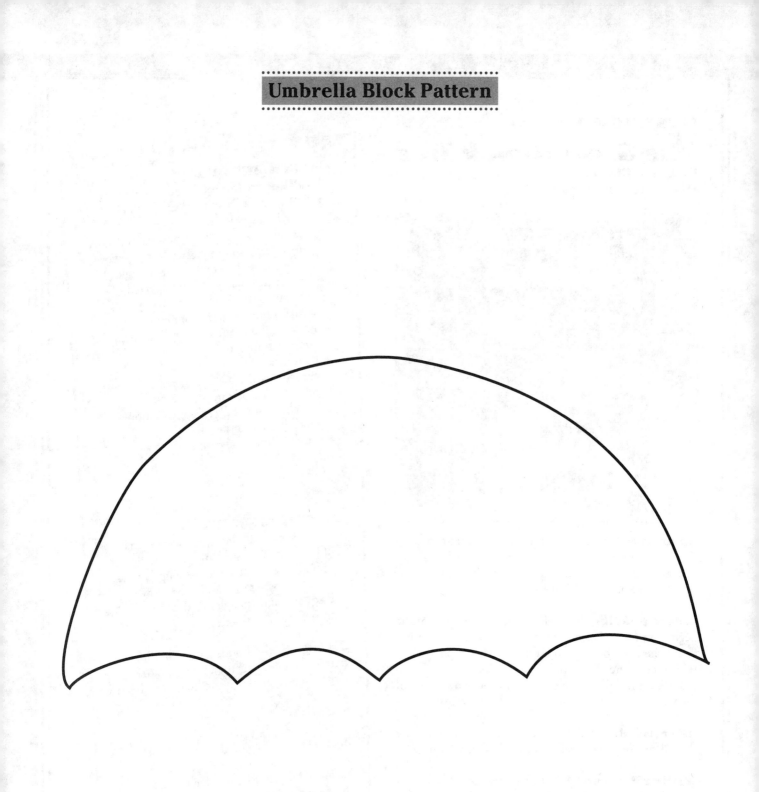

LET'S READ (Selection B)

Flower Garden
by Eve Bunting
(Harcourt Brace, 1994)

Summary: In this easy-to-read, rhyming picture book, a small girl and her father buy flowering plants, then hurry home to plant them in a flower box for her mother's birthday. Vibrant colors bring the story and flowers to life.

Before Reading: Ask children: Have you ever made a flower box or planted a garden? What did you plant? Explain to children that spring is usually the time when people plant seeds and when flowers bloom.

After Reading: Have children think about what they would plant if they had their own flower box or garden.

Writing Prompts: Ask students to complete one of the following sentences to include in their paper quilt:

> • I would plant _____ in my garden because _____.
>
> • I would give _____ to _____
> from my garden because _____.

Don't Stop Now!

Plant your very own flower box in the classroom. Discuss with children the kind of flowers they would like to buy. Then take children on a field trip to a nearby flower store to buy seeds, a flower box, soil, and other potting needs (trowel, gloves, etc.). After you plant the seeds, assign different children to water the plants as needed.

MAKING THE QUILT
You'll need (for each student):

◆ Philadelphia Pavements Quilt Block pattern, page 58
◆ Three 2-inch squares of flower-print wrapping paper (Cut two squares in half to form four triangles.)
◆ Six 2-inch squares of yellow or magenta construction paper* (Cut two squares in half to form four triangles.)
◆ Four 1/2-inch squares of yellow or magenta construction paper
◆ Flower Block pattern, page 62, cut from white paper and yellow or magenta construction paper
◆ 7-inch square of yellow or magenta construction paper (for background)
◆ Two leaves, page 62, cut from green construction paper
◆ Large button
◆ Glue

*Give half the class yellow construction paper, and the other half, magenta.

PIECE IT TOGETHER

1. To make the Philadelphia Pavements Quilt Block, have students glue the flower-print squares and triangles to the spaces numbered "1," and the yellow or magenta squares and triangles to the spaces numbered "2."

2. Give each child both Flower Block patterns stapled together. Then have the children write their response to the literature (from Writing Prompts, left) on the white flower.

3. Have children glue the back of the white flower to the yellow or magenta background square. Then have them glue the button to the flower's center. Finally, have students glue the leaves to the flower.

4. Assemble the class quilt. (See page 7 for instructions.)

JUNE

What better way to end the school year than to celebrate

your students and their accomplishments. Children will feel

empowered by Nancy Carlson's *I Like Me*.

Debra Frasier's *On the Day You Were Born* will introduce kids

to the wonders of nature as the world gets ready to welcome them.

◆

Simple in its design, the year-end quilt

makes your students the centerpiece.

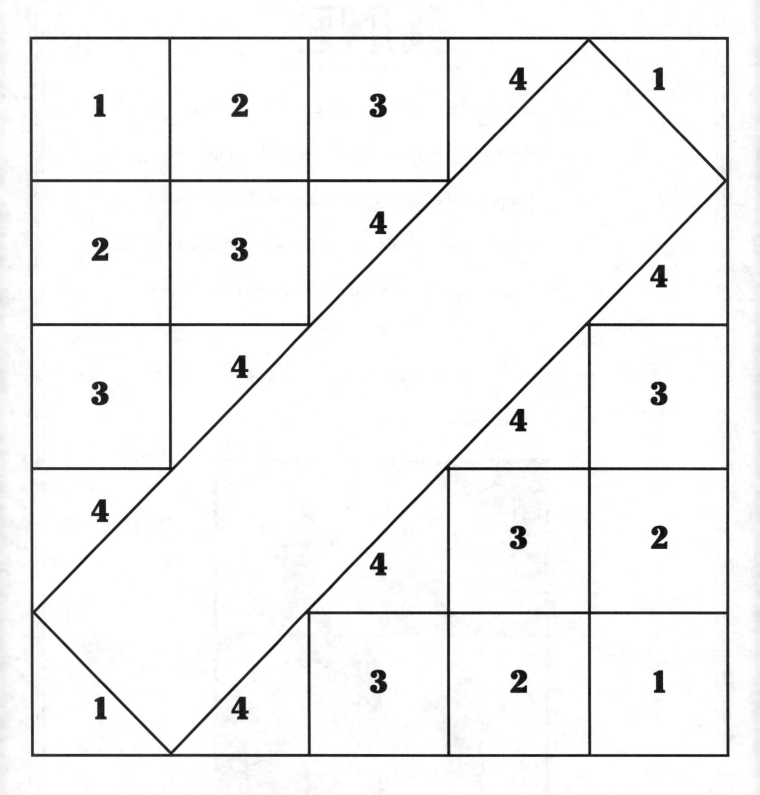

LET'S READ (Selection A)

I Like Me
by Nancy Carlson
(Puffin, 1990)

Summary: A little pig shares with readers the joys of being herself. This inspirational book emphasizes the importance of feeling good about oneself, even during sad times and bad times.

Before Reading: Have children name three things they are good at. Then invite them to share three mistakes they have made recently. Ask: How do you feel when you make mistakes? Remind the children that it's okay to make mistakes—it's one of the many ways we learn about life.

After Reading: Ask children: What things do you like to do? What things are you most proud of?

Instead of having the children complete writing prompts, have them draw six things they like to do or are proud of in the Pictograph Block (page 66).

Don't Stop Now!
Self-esteem can be gained not only by appreciating yourself, but by learning what others like about you. Have students sit in a circle. Going clockwise, invite each student to name one thing they really like about

the child sitting to their right. After everyone has had their turn, go around the circle again, and have each child repeat what was said about them.

MAKING THE QUILT
You'll need (for each student):
◆ Friendship Quilt Block pattern, page 64
◆ Seventeen 1 1/2-inch squares of four different-color construction paper (3 squares of one color, 4 squares of a second color, 6 squares of a third color, and 4 squares of a fourth color. Cut one square of the first color in half to make two triangles. Cut all squares of the fourth color in half to make eight triangles.)
◆ Pictograph Block pattern, page 66
◆ Child Block pattern, page 67, cut from skin-color felt (Have a range of different-color felt handy to reflect the diversity of students.)
◆ Colored pencils
◆ Glue

PIECE IT TOGETHER
1. To make the Friendship Quilt Block, have students choose one color for the spaces numbered "1," a second color for the spaces numbered "2," and so on. Have them glue the squares and triangles onto the quilt block. Invite children to write their names in the white rectangular space at the center of the quilt block.

2. Encourage children to draw six pictures of things they like to do or are proud of on the Pictograph Block.

3. Invite children to select a skin-color felt child that they feel best represents themselves. Have them glue the child to the center space on the Pictograph.

4. Assemble the class quilt. (See page 7 for instructions.)

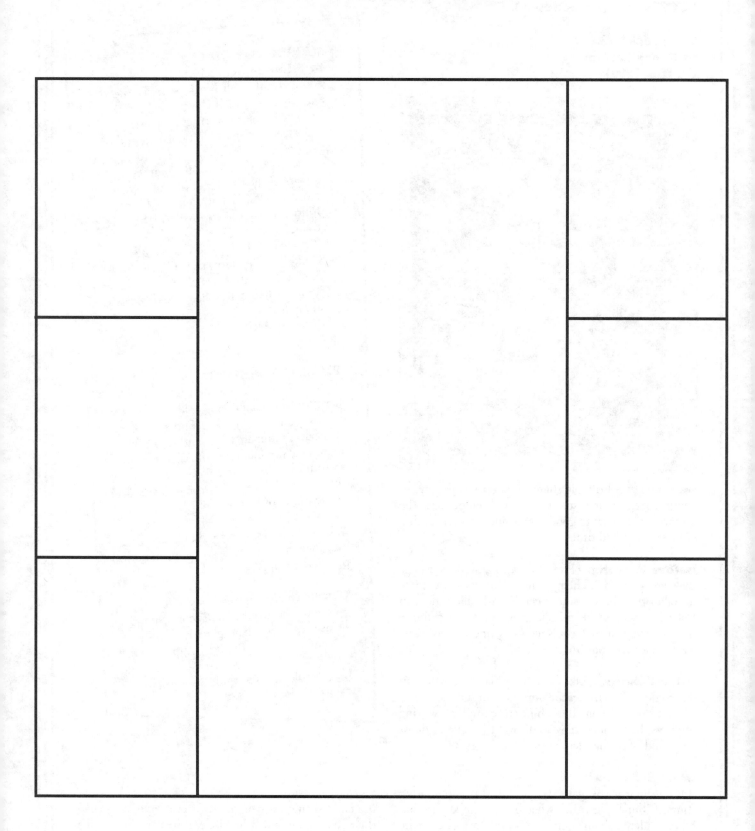

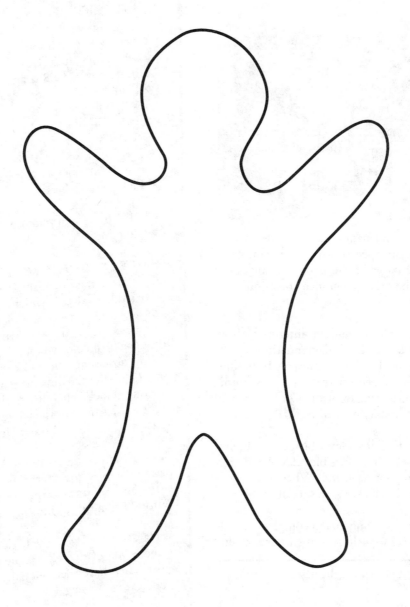

LET'S READ (Selection B)

On the Day You Were Born

by Debra Fasier
(Harcourt Brace, 1991)

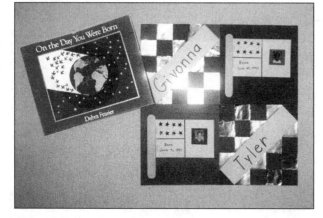

Summary: Science and nature come to life in this poetic telling of what happened "on the day you were born." The last few pages of the book explain tides, migration, gravity, and other phenomena mentioned in the book.

Before Reading: Have children interview their parents about their birth: What day and time was I born? What was the weather like? Besides my birth, did anything else special happen on the day I was born? Then invite children to bring in pictures of themselves as babies and share the story of their birth.

After Reading: Children love birthdays. Invite children to talk about their favorite birthday. Ask them: Which birthday is your favorite? What happened during this birthday that makes it so special?

Writing Prompts: Ask students to complete one of the following sentences to include in their paper quilt:

> • I like to _____ to celebrate the day I was born.
>
> • I am special because _____.

Don't Stop Now!

The birth of a child adds another branch to a family tree. Have children interview their parents to find out who belongs in their family tree. If possible, have children go back at least three generations. Create a template of a family tree for children to fill in.

MAKING THE QUILT
You'll need (for each student):

◆ Friendship Quilt Block pattern, page 64
◆ Nine 1 1/2-inch squares of red and blue construction paper (Three squares of one color and 6 squares of the other. Cut one square of the first color in half to make 2 triangles.)
◆ Four 1 1/2-inch squares of gold wrapping paper (Cut each square in half to make 8 triangles.)
◆ Four 1 1/2-inch squares of silver wrapping paper
◆ Two Flag Block patterns, page 69, cut from white paper
◆ 7 1/2-inch square of red or blue construction paper (for background)
◆ Eight star stickers
◆ Popsicle stick
◆ 1 1/2-by-2-inch photo of your student
◆ Glue

PIECE IT TOGETHER

1. To make the Friendship Quilt Block, have students decide which color construction paper to use for the spaces numbered "1" and "3." Then have them decide which color wrapping paper to use for the spaces numbered "2" and "4." Have them glue the squares and triangles onto the quilt block. Then invite children to write their names in the white rectangular space at the center of the quilt block.

2. Give each child both Flag Block patterns stapled together. Have children write their response to the literature (from Writing Prompts, left) on the second flag.

3. Have students glue the back of the flag to the center of the red or blue background paper. Then have them glue the popsicle stick next to the flag.

4. Have children stick the stars to the upper left-hand section of the flag, and write their birth dates below it. Finally, have children glue their photos on the right-hand section of the flag.

5. Assemble the class quilt. (See page 7 for instructions.)

Additional Books
Here are more books you can use with your month-by-month quilts:

September
Sweet Clara and the Freedom Quilt by Deborah Hopkinson
(Random House, 1995)

The Boy and the Quilt by Shirley Kurtz
(Goodbooks, 1991)

Eight Hands Round by Ann Whitford Paul
(HarperTrophy, 1996)

The Patchwork Quilt by Valerie Flournoy
(Dutton, 1985)

October
The 13 Nights of Halloween by Rebecca Dickinson
(Cartwheel Books, 1996)

Scary, Scary Halloween by Eve Bunting
(Clarion, 1986)

The Bat Jamboree by Kathi Appelt
(William Morrow, 1996)

Bats: Creatures of the Night by Joyce Milton
(Price Stern Sloan, 1993)

November
Giving Thanks: A Native American Good Morning Message by Jake Swamp
(Lee & Low Books, 1997)

Legend of the Bluebonnet by Tomie dePaola
(Putnam, 1986)

Mud Pony retold by Caron Lee Cohen
(Scholastic, 1992)

Rainbow Crow: A Lenape Tale by Nancy Van Laan
(Knopf, 1991)

December
Messy Bessey's Holidays by Patricia McKissack
(Children's Press, 1999)

Elijah's Angel: A Story for Chanukah and Christmas by Michael J. Rosen
(Harcourt Brace, 1997)

Christmas at Long Pond by William T. George
(Mulberry Books, 1996)

Owl Moon by Jane Yolen
(Philomel, 1987)

January
Snowballs by Lois Elhert
(Voyager Picture Book, 1999)

The Black Snowman by Phil Mendez
(Scholastic, 1991)

The Jacket I Wear in the Snow by Shirley Neitzel
(Mulberry Books, 1994)

Snow Day! By Barbara M. Joosse
(Clarion Books, 1995)

February
I Love You With All My Heart by Noris Kern
(Chronicle Books, 1998)

Guess How Much I Love You by Sam McBratney
(Candlewick Press, 1995)

If You Grew Up With Abraham Lincoln by Ann McGovern
(Scholastic, 1976)

Abe Lincoln's Hat by Martha Brenner
(Random House, 1994)

March
The Mitten by Alvin Tresselt
(William Morrow, 1964)

The Hat by Jan Brett
(Putnam, 1997)

Jamie O'Rourke and the Big Potato by Tomie dePaola
(Putnam, 1992)

Leprechaun Gold by Teresa Bateman
(Holiday House, 1998)

April
The Tale of Peter Rabbit by Beatrix Potter
(Little Simon Books, 1990)

Hopper Hunts for Spring by Marcus Pfister
(North South Books, 1992)

Tam's Slipper by Janet Polazzo-Craig
(Troll, 1997)

Rechenka's Eggs by Patricia Polacco
(Putnam, 1988)

May
Rain Forest by Helen Cowcher
(Farrar Straus & Giroux, 1988)

Rain Forest Babies by Kathy Darling
(Walker & Co., 1997)

The Carrot Seed by Ruth Krauss
(HarperTrophy, 1989)

Jack's Garden by Henry Cole
(Mulberry, 1997)

June
I Like Being Me by Judy Lalli
(Free Spirit, 1997)

Just Because I Am: A Child's Book of Affirmation by Lauren Murphy Payne
(Free Spirit, 1994)

Sometimes I Feel Like a Mouse: A Book About Feelings by Jeanne Modesitt
(Scholastic, 1996)

A Bad Case of Stripes by David Shannon
(Scholastic, 1998)